OFFENSE NOT DEFENSE

Surviving In Your Purpose

By Nicole Roshelle

Copyright © By DLL Publishing, LLC

All Rights Reserved

November 2016

This book is dedicated to anyone who has experienced a loss, and ultimately lost themselves. If you've grieved after a death, divorce, job loss, separation, etc., this book is dedicated to you! Follow my journey and use it as the inspiration, motivation, and encouragement needed to positively work through your grief, and gain the strength you will need in the fight to take back your life! Your sanity depends on it!

Nicole Roshelle

Table of Contents

Introduction 7

In The Beginning 11
So Young, So Inexperienced, So Lost 21

I Am…..Because *GOD* Is! 25
And The Dream Begins...29

Plans For The Future 33
Senior Year 37

A Not So Happy Holiday 41

    Tuesday, November 29, 2011   45
    Wednesday, November 30, 2011   47
    Thursday, December 1, 2011   55
    Friday, December 2, 2011   63
    Tuesday, December 6, 2011   75
    Wednesday, December 7, 2011   79
    Thursday, December 8, 2011   83

The Day After..93

The Aftermath...97
Me, Myself, & I 101

Stuck In Grief..107
Finding Purpose In My Pain 113
March 2016..117
Healing 125

Present Day 139

According to the statistics, I am not supposed to be here right now. I've been through a lot in my life, and yet I've survived. Where I'm from, a lot of people don't make it out. They don't survive and they succumb to their circumstances. I'm so blessed to be able to not only have a story to tell, but to have the courage to tell it. This is for those who think they can't make it, those who think they aren't good enough, those who believe it when people tell them that they will never be able to do this or that, and those like myself who never dream big enough! I have made a lot of mistakes in my life, but I've also learned from them. That is what life is about; learning from our experiences while always being open to growth. Don't ever put limits on yourself! If you dream it, you can do it!

"For the Lord giveth wisdom: out of his mouth cometh knowledge and understanding." (Proverbs 2 v. 6)

In The Beginning

Why don't I take you back for a moment, and tell you a little more about myself. My name is Nicole; people call me "Nikki", or "Nikki Lew". It's 2011, and at this time, I am a 32 year old mother of 1. Born December 11, 1978, in the city of Richmond, raised in the heart of what some may call the "hood", Highland Park. As the product of two teenaged, unwed parents, the cards were stacked against me. My mother was 15, and my father about 17. Even as a teenaged mother, my mom stayed in school and graduated on time. My dad was a different story. He is what we would call a "street" dude, in other words, a born hustler! Although it wasn't perfect, my childhood was awesome, and it felt perfect to me. At the age of about 9, we left Highland Park and moved to the projects, Jackson Ward. My father hustled and my mother worked. His hustling afforded me a life that many kids my age could never dream of! Even though we lived in the projects, we didn't live like most of the people in our neighborhood. I had my own room where I slept in a brass bed that I didn't have to share with anyone! We had color televisions in every room, electronics, furnishings, you name it, and we had it!

At that age, I didn't really understand that how we lived wasn't how everyone lived. I would visit my friends and some may not have furniture or they had to share clothes with their siblings. Some didn't even live with their fathers. Even though we lived in the projects, it didn't feel that way as a child. You don't understand that this is low income or supposedly "less than". It's just home to you, it's your neighborhood. But my dad always told me to appreciate and take care of the things I had. He would always say, "Everyone doesn't live like this, most of your friends have to share a room with their sisters and brothers, some even share a bed!" He didn't say that to make me feel special, he said that to make me understand that he provided a life for us that could be taken away at any time. He may not have known it at the time, but that humbled me. He never allowed me to feel like I was better because I had more or dressed different; he made sure I understood this was a life of privilege. A lot of older people in the neighborhood knew me because of my dad; he was the guy that knew everybody! We rode around in nice cars and always had the latest and greatest. I did not really understand it all at such a young age, it just seemed normal to me. But, there are consequences to hustling, and because of that, he spent a lot of time incarcerated. Raised by my grandparents, my mother, and my mostly absent father, I must say that even though there were some tough times, I wouldn't change a thing! But as I've matured, I've realized the impact my father has had on my life is greater than I could've imagined. He has taught me so much, unintentionally. Because of him, I not only have book sense, but I have street sense. When you are the child of a hustler, you see and hear things that a child should never see or hear. In hindsight, I've realized that those experiences have made me better. I can make a dollar out of 15 cents, spot a scam a mile away, and survive on my own, without needing to depend on a man! I was, and will always be a daddy's girl, but he raised me to be as sufficient as any man I encounter. He may not even realize it himself, but he is why I've learned to survive! There are so many things that I would love to change about my father, but at the end of the day, if he wasn't himself, I wouldn't be myself. I look at my siblings sometimes and wish they could have experienced the same journey as I. I feel like it would have molded them differently, their skin would be just a tad bit thicker. It is always a great thing to be able to raise your children in the best of neighborhoods and have them attend the best schools. But in this game called life, survival skills will be required! Sometimes when children are sheltered and haven't had certain life experiences, they become adults who are sheltered. They face situations in life unequipped with the skill set to survive. Even to this day my father is that same guy, he still has that "hustler's spirit"! I love him for raising me with that same spirit that still lies within me today.

As a child, I was a very quiet kid, did well in school, and spent a lot of time alone because I was an only child. At the age of ten, all of that changed, I became a big sister! I always wondered why my parents waited ten whole years to have another child. I can only assume it wasn't at all planned! As time went on, I became more of a mother than a big sister. With our mother working two and three jobs and our father usually on a hiatus, I was the only person to fill the void. I spent a lot of time caring for my sister, I basically raised her. That can be a bit stressful for someone at such a young age, especially when I became a mother myself. Yes, I was a teen mother. My parents had me at a young age, and 15 years later, history would repeat itself! On February 10, 1994 at 5:47pm, weighing in at 5lbs and 14 oz., D'Ashawn Leon Lewis was born. I named him "Leon" after my dad. That is his middle name, and also his father's middle name, and now the middle name of my son! And at that very moment, my life changed forever. At only 15 years old, I was someone's mother! I was responsible for the well-being of this little innocent life! For some reason, *GOD* chose me!

"He that hath the son hath life; and he that hath not the Son of GOD hath not life." (1 John 5 v. 12)

Thankfully *GOD* provided me with a solid family structure and the motivation to not become a victim of my circumstance. When you're that age, everyone expects you to follow the "norm". They expect you not to graduate, to continue to have babies out of wedlock, become dependent on the government and not pursue any dreams or reach any goals. But not I, I had other plans!! And thankfully I was supported by a family who wouldn't allow me to settle for less. During my pregnancy, I experienced complications and was taken out of school and placed on bed rest, I was only in the 10th grade at this time. To make sure I stayed on track, a tutor was provided and visited me every Tuesday. She was the most boring teacher I had ever had! I absolutely hated those weekly visits! But now I look back and appreciate that teacher! She pushed me and didn't allow me to slack off or fall behind. Because of her, I graduated on time and with my class! Not in summer school, night school, or an adult education program. Not only did I graduate on time, I graduated with offers to join the U. S. Navy. But as a new mother, I sacrificed those dreams because I didn't want to leave my son. I graduated high school in 1996, all while working and being a full time mom. My class load during my senior year consisted of only 4 classes, so I only had school for a half day, so I was able to work the other half of the day. Giving up was never an option for me!

So Young,

So Inexperienced,

So Lost

Even though I did benefit from government assistance at some point, I never depended on it; I used it as a stepping stone to push me further. Since I was unable to join the service, I decided to pursue another passion, cosmetology. I started cosmetology school Sept of 1996 and graduated in May of 1997. During this time, I met a guy who was much older. When I look back now, I can only think of how gullible I was!! So young, so inexperienced, and so lost, I allowed this person to come into my life and turn it upside down. For the longest time I carried around so much hatred for him, I had to learn to let go of what was and appreciate what is! He said all the right things, made all the right moves, made me feel like I had hit the lottery! He cared for my son as if he was his own; all while cheating, lying, and being abusive. Somehow he was able to turn my own family against me. They always took his word over mines, took his side over mines, and always seem to make me feel like I was the trouble maker. I can remember so many times where there was arguing and fighting, and I had to suffer alone, no one to turn to, no one to call, no one to rescue me. There was one incident where we argued about something, I can't remember exactly what, but it turned into an altercation. He took his two hands, placed them around my throat, and forced me on top of a dresser. Yes, he put me on top of a dresser with only his two hands around my neck! The closest thing I could grab was a telephone. This was back when we all still used house phones and cell phones were almost non-existent. I took the phone and constantly hit him with it until he finally let me go. Once he let me go, I ran out to the nearest phone booth and to call the police. You may wonder where my son was during all of this, he was right there!! He was only about 2 years old at the time, having to witness it all. By the time I made it back to the house, the police had arrived. Because I hit him with the phone, he had a large, open place on his chest. Because of this, the police advised me that they could arrest me because he had physical evidence of abuse, as where I did not. Of course he did not press charges, but at that moment, I realized that my life was spiraling out of control. I had become so numb to what was going in my life that the abuse started not to faze me any longer. There was another time where we had an argument about something, and he threw a remote control at me. The remote hit me directly in the eye. To this very day, I still have a mark from that remote control. My eye was swollen and black, and yet I got up the next day, took my son to the babysitter, and went to work. At the time I worked at the customer service desk in a retail store, so I was the first person the customers saw as they entered the store. I stood there my entire shift as if I looked like a beauty queen. The stares I received that day from customers and co-workers let me know that I had given up. I literally let someone beat the life out of me.

I Am.....Because GOD Is!

But because *GOD* doesn't give up on us, my life started to change. I received a letter stating that I had been approved for my first apartment; I was currently still living at home. This was it, this was my opportunity to break free and start a new life on my own. When it came time to move into my new apartment, I made it clear that it would just be my son and I. Because my mother was also moving, it made it a little easier to break away from him. By this time I had my own car and was about to finish cosmetology school. It was all coming together for me. Even though these positive things were happening, it still took a while for me to break free from that relationship. When you're in that type of relationship, it tears you down. You lose yourself, your worth, your self-confidence, your drive; you literally began to lose your mind! I was in such a dark place. I had thoughts of suicide, even though I never acted on them, I did have those thoughts. For some reason I felt like that was my only way out, the only way I would find some sort of peace in my life. I quickly realized that I had something to live for, my son. He needed me, he needed me to make life different and allow him the opportunities I missed out on.

My first apartment wasn't in the best of neighborhoods, but it was mine. If you're patient, and continue to put in the work, the blessings will flow. I can remember my neighbors shooting at one another and my son and I having to lie down on the floor. It was the scariest feeling to hear those gunshots so close and to know that your baby could be hit by one of them. Shortly after that, I received a letter stating that an apartment, where I had been on the waiting list, was now ready for me! This apartment was in a much better neighborhood, and again, my prayers had been answered! Not only was I moving to a better neighborhood, but I also was offered a higher paying position at work. At the time I worked as a bank teller, and moved up to a customer service representative. There were so many times that I could have given up, but I didn't. So many times where I could have settled, but I wasn't satisfied, I wanted more, even in my darkest hour, my heart desired more! Throughout the years I managed to maintain a steady job while raising my son. I suffered with what I now know to be anxiety. I felt as though I was able to successfully move forward from that abusive relationship and get on with my life, not understanding that the anxiety was a souvenir. This is something I would never discuss until now. Outside of that, I feel like my son had a pretty normal childhood. I did my best to make sure of it. I worked a lot, but I made sure that he was well taken care of and in a stable environment. Even though I love my mother and appreciate her, I didn't want him to have the same experiences I did. I spent a lot of time alone, caring for myself and my sister because she spent a lot of time away from home. I tried to make sure that if he wasn't with me, he was with my grandparents or in some type of program for kids. If I worked late and got off at midnight or later, I still would pick him up and take him home. I was a very "hands on" mother, very in tune to what was going on with my child and how he felt about certain things. Sometimes as adults we don't realize how our lifestyles can affect our children; I was really careful and did my best to make the right decisions for the both of us.

And The Dream Begins

At the age of about 5 years old I signed my son up for flag football, this would change his life forever. He loved the sport of football. He started out playing for a recreational team; he played from the age of 5 until about 14 years old when he started to play for his high school team. He had those NFL dreams, just like every young kid who falls in love with football! He planned to attend the University of Miami and become a HURRICANE! I did my best to keep him on the right path and working towards his goals. As parents, we must understand that when we decide to become parents, we forfeit our right to be individuals. We are required to become selfless and put our children before ourselves. Sacrifice becomes the story of our lives. All those evening practices and early morning games were sacrifices I made to make sure that he was able to do something that he not only loved, but it kept him focused, motivated, and lessened his chances of becoming a statistic. I understand that it is hard to pay fees, work full time, get dinner on the table after leaving the practice field at 8 or 9 pm, get up early on Saturday mornings and spend the better part of your day at the football field supporting the teams, but in the end, it's worth it. It was worth me bouncing a few checks to make sure his fees were paid and his fundraiser money was on time. It was worth it to travel from this field to that field and watch him play against teams of all different races, talents, and neighborhoods. I don't regret buying football pictures, volunteering my time at the concession stand, or being the team mom providing snacks for the team after the game. I loved every moment of it!! I now understand that at any time our children can be taken away from us. We must appreciate every moment we have with our children and support every activity they want to participate in. We have to understand that time is precious and not promised. I can remember hearing parents complain about practice times, game times, volunteering, etc., and sometimes, I was one of those parents. But I quickly realized that the sacrifice was small compared to the payoff in the end. Parents support your kids, make the sacrifice. You just never know what the end result could be. Support their dreams; encourage them to live life to their full potential. All they have to do is imagine it, and it can be! Motivate them to work hard and stay focused on their goals. There are so many distractions and kids can get off course. It is our duty as parents to inspire them to be successful and set the example of excellence.

Plans For The Future

In 2010, I rekindled an old flame. We spent time together, worked on our differences, and decided we would get married. Even though he and I had been off and on in our relationship for a few years, he always remained a constant in D'Ashawn's life. I always appreciated the relationship they had, whether he and I were together or not, he remained a positive father figure in my son's life. In deciding to get married, we also had to make the decision to live together, my son and I moving into his home with his children. This was a first for me; I had never moved into someone else's home, I always had my own place with my son. I knew this would be a challenge, but we were willing to work through it to start our new life together. We actually moved together in May of 2011. I didn't really expect any issues with the kids because they already had some sort of relationship with one another; we just had to now figure out how we all would live as one and under one roof. Things seemed to progress slowly, there were some challenges, but the kids were truly becoming closer than ever. I believe, for us as parents, that was the most important thing. As the fall approaches, my son prepares to start his senior year of high school. Currently I work in corporate

America and operate my own business as a licensed cosmetologist. At the time, I absolutely hated my corporate job, but getting my son through high school and on to college motivated me to keep pushing forward until something better came along. As for my son, he is now a 17 year old high school senior who is active in sports, football and track. He goes by many aliases, "Sapp", "D. Lewiz", "D. Lew", but to us, he was just "D'A". He plays on the varsity football team and does shot put for the track team. He is dead set on attending the college of his dreams, but his G.P.A. needs some work. He has taken SAT prep classes to increase his chances of successfully completing the SAT test, but now needs to focus on a plan to increase his GPA, and to better his chances of being accepted into the school of his choice. So to increase his chances of acceptance, we decided that a 2 year college in Philadelphia was the first stop he needed to make in order to reach his goal.

Senior Year

It is now the fall of 2011, October to be exact, and my son and I are hitting the highway! We're leaving Richmond, VA and traveling to Philly, PA to visit a college he is hoping to attend next fall. Since this is his senior year, we have planned to visit a number of college campuses. I don't know if it was because it was the first school, or if he just knew this was the school for him, but this trip meant everything to us. He was so excited, and if you know my son, the only thing he was ever excited about was football or a new dance move. We had so much time to bond and enjoy quality time with one another. I enjoyed seeing him engaged in the next phase of his life, asking questions, picking out classes, making decisions without my help; just becoming an adult. I cherished those moments; it would be the last time we would travel together. During the visit we toured the grounds, visited the dorms, and attended an orientation for the football team. I had never seen him like this! He was like a big kid, just excited to see what was next, wearing the biggest smile the entire day. He was always very laid back, the type of guy that took everything in stride. He was starting to make plans and get enthused about his future. It was like he could see the light at the end of the tunnel, like he was starting to realize how all the hard work could pay off. After our exciting getaway, the next thing on our agenda is to visit the department of motor vehicles. If you know my son, you know he walks *EVERYWHERE*! So getting him to get his driver's license was like pulling teeth! I finally got him to take the test. We go in; he started the test, got one sign incorrect, and failed instantly! Even though *he* failed, I seemed to be the only one concerned. He continued to study the driver's manual, but quickly let me know that getting his license was the least of his worries. As a compromise, he did agree to at least go back to get an identification card. About a week later his card arrives, and more college visits are on our agenda.

Thanksgiving is approaching, so my then fiancé and I, we will call him "Robert"; decide to host our families for the first time ever; nine kids, grandparents, parents, siblings, and friends all under one roof. This was our way to bring everyone together. We didn't realize at the time that it was really the divine order of things. It would turn out to be the last time that we would all be together as a family, the last time that many of them would see my son alive again. We returned from the trip and the next day his SAT results came in, he scored a 1010! A 340 in critical reading, 360 in math, and a 310 in writing! I was so proud of him! I have never even attempted to take the SATs in my entire life, and yet my son studied, took SAT prep classes, and aced it!

A Not So Happy Holiday

Shortly before the holiday, as usual, my son and I head out. I take him to school, and then I head to work. Well this particular morning he walked in front of me to cross the street. As always, he has his headphones in, and his iPod is blasting! Oblivious to what is going on around him, he crosses the street as a truck is coming, but he never sees the truck. Luckily the truck driver did see him and was able to slow down. I'm yelling and screaming his name, waving my hands, but he never hears or sees me!! The driver is beeping his horn; he still doesn't hear a thing! He makes it safely across the street and I just lose it! I was so shaken up by what I had just witnessed! I yelled at him the entire ride to school. And being his usual carefree self, he was unbothered. He apologized, but in his typical nonchalant tone.

He was so laid back, no urgency about anything! Everything with him was always "chill". I loved that about him, even though sometimes it drove me crazy! I was the fire, and he was the cool, calm ocean. Sagittarius and Aquarius! All that I could think of was him being run over by this truck, right in front of me! We always got on him about those headphones and how loud he would always have them. He wore those headphones 24/7! But this day, they almost cost him his life! At the time, I had no idea what all of this meant, I just knew it scared me to death!

*Tuesday,
November 29, 2011*

The holiday was a success and we're getting back to our daily routines. As always, I woke up my son, took him to school, and I headed to work. The day started out normal, but once I got to work, it changed drastically! For some odd reason, I continuously cried the entire day! For my full eight hour shift I cried, and cried, and cried! Every chance I had, I would call Robert crying like a baby! I just remember this feeling of devastation and depression that came over me. At the time I felt it was because I was so unhappy with my job, but I would later realize that it was something much worse than that.

*Wednesday,
November 30, 2011*

As usual, I wake D'A up for school, and he gets dressed listening to one of his favorite songs. "Cause I Love You" by Lenny Williams. Even though he was only 17, he had what the old folks would call an "old soul". We arrive at the school, he gets out, and like always, I say "I love you" and he says, "Love you too". He shuts the car door, and that is the last time I see him alive. I'm off today because I have an appointment later in the day concerning a new job. The day goes by and I finish my appointment earlier than expected, about 5:45pm. It's too early to pick D'A up from track practice; he's usually not ready until about 7pm. But something in my spirit tells me to text him and let him know that I would be at the school to pick him up, but instead I just head home and wait for him to text or call me. Time goes by, and before I know it, it is now 8 pm. I haven't heard from D'A at all. I call Robert, and he hasn't heard from him either. I text my brother to see if he's heard from him, usually after practice he would walk to my brother's house and wait for someone to pick him up, he hasn't heard from him either. This didn't sit well with me because this wasn't like him. I decided to head towards the school. I figured maybe he was hanging out in the area with some of his team mates. I get off the interstate exit and police are everywhere!! The street is blocked from one end to the other. I wasn't able to go directly into the area I needed to because the police had it blocked off. So I pull into the parking lot of a fast food restaurant which sits on the corner. As I pull in, my brother calls and says someone asked him was he okay because there was an accident in the area where he lives; he lived in walking distance of the school. I let him know that I was there and that something did seem to be going on, but I wasn't sure what. My brother has a roommate, so I call him to see if he's seen D'A. He said he hadn't seen him, and as a matter of fact, it didn't seem as if he had been to the apartment at all that day. I tell him that I'm in the parking lot, and he walks over. As he approaches my car, a news reporter, who had been sitting in the van next to me, says "Is this the mother?" I respond, "Whose mother?" I'm clueless as to what this woman is talking about and why she is talking to me! I shut my car door, and she walks away. We sit there for a while and Robert calls to tell me he is on the way. I let him know where I'm parked and why. Still clueless as to what is going on and where my son is! I hear a weird tone in his voice, but I say nothing. He arrives and I let him know we still haven't heard from D'A. So he walks further down the street and sees D'Ashawn's football coach standing on the corner. Now I'm thinking to myself, well what in the world is he doing out here? Still not comprehending or realizing what is going on around me. Robert comes back and tells me that D'A has been in an accident. I scream and hop over into the passenger side of the car. I start to call my mother and he says, "What are you doing?" I say, "We need to go! You drive!!! We need to go now!! Why are we still sitting here??? Where are the ambulances?? WHAT IS GOING ON??" He just walks away again. He comes back, and does not have to say one word!! Silence. Just the look on his face told me that my world had ended in just the blink of an eye! I fell to the pavement of the parking lot screaming like my heart had just been ripped out of my chest!! Robert gets me off the ground and into the car. All I can say is…"I want to go home." Before we leave the scene, my mother calls back. I have to tell her what was just told to me, but I can't form the words. I just simply say, "Ma, he's gone." I hear her belt out a loud scream and I just pass the phone to Robert.

He confirms, and she and my grandmother say they are on their way to the scene. I would find out later that the weird tone in Robert's voice earlier was because he had received a call while on his way to the scene from D'Ashawn's football coach. He'd called to tell him about the accident, he just didn't have the heart to tell me. Even though my son had his identification card in his wallet, the same identification card I had to beg him to get, his coach still had to visually identify him. The same identification card he had no interest in getting is ultimately what was used to identify him. It's funny because that card had only arrived about a week or so before the accident. Sometime later I would ask his football coach how D'Ashawn looked, he would say to me, "you don't really want to know that".

We head home and have to face the task of telling our other children the news. We arrive home and no one is there but Robert's oldest daughter. She's in her room with the door shut. Watching him walk toward that room door to tell her that he was gone, it seemed as if he was walking in slow motion, like it would take him 10 hours to get there. He walks in, and instantly she says, "Daddy, what is going on?" "Why is everyone calling me saying D'Ashawn is dead?" The tone in her voice lets me know that she didn't believe it could be true, not for one second! I didn't hear his response, but the next thing I heard still gives me chills to this day! I will never in all my years of living forget the way she screamed. She yelled *NO* so loud you could hear and feel the pain in her voice. For a moment, I felt as if I was on pause. I felt her hurt from the hallway! She was inconsolable! All he could do was close the door and allow her to grieve. This was just the beginning, the beginning of a roller coaster ride that had become our lives. As we headed to our bedroom, it all began to flash across the television screen. Each news channel is covering the teenaged high school student who was fatally struck by a car on Airport Drive. We sat there watching as if it wasn't about our son, as if it weren't real. We just kept saying to each other, "this can't be real!" I think for a moment we were both in such a state of shock and disbelief that we didn't comprehend what was actually going on around us. The phones were ringing off the hook and the people were starting to arrive. The only people we had a chance to tell were those with us on the scene; his daughter, my mother, and my grandmother. Some way, somehow, everyone found out and flocked to our doorstep. We later found out that the news of his death had been all over social media since the accident happened, around 6:15pm! Students, who were also on the scene, walking home from practice as well, witnessed the accident. *R.I.P. D. LEW* would flood social media sites well on into the next day, the next week, the next month, and years to come.

*Thursday,
December 1, 2011*

The calls and texts continue to roll in. My family and I are still trying to process what has transpired over the last few hours. At about 4am my phone rings, I answer, and there is a woman on the other end asking for the parents of D'Ashawn Leon Lewis. I advise her that I'm his mother and she proceeds to say this is _____ calling to ask if your son was an organ donor. I'm not totally in my right mind, but I actually can't believe what I am hearing! I ask her to repeat herself, and she says it again! I say to her "ma'am, do you realize my son just died a few hours ago?" "It hasn't even been 24 hours yet!" She says that she is sorry for my lost, "but we only have a small window of time to make this decision." Sensing my frustration, Robert takes the phone and continues the conversation. He asks her to give us a few hours, and to call back around 11am. She would continue to constantly call throughout the day until I finally said NO!! "We will not be making any organ donations!" "You can't harvest his organs!" Still, even today, I have regrets about making that decision! I know the benefits of organ donation and how our loss could have been a blessing to someone else. But at that very moment, during that time, your head is not in the right place. You're totally having an out of body experience. I literally felt as if I was in a fog!! So much was going on around me and it wasn't sinking in that I was preparing to bury my son. Even though I had a very strong support system, I still struggled with the reality that was my life at that time.

The day seemed to drag by. Between the constant visits from family members and loved ones, and the steady stream of calls and text messages, I felt overwhelmed, anxious, confused, and empty. Unfortunately, Robert and I had recently been through this same situation only nine months before. In February 2011 we lost his sister to pancreatic cancer. Although we mourned the loss of her, this loss somehow was different. I can't explain it because of course they were both devastating, but this was just different. Robert and I were very private people, and this seemed to make our very private life, *VERY public!* The accident and death of D'Ashawn seemed to take on a life of its own. Between the constant news coverage on all of the local stations, several articles in the local newspaper, and of course the 24/7 flood of social media posts, you would think that my family and I would have endured enough during our time of grieving. But oh no, not only did all three of the major local news stations appear at our front door unannounced, they expected an interview! All I could think to myself was how inconsiderate and thoughtless could you be to have the nerve to take the time out of your day to disturb a grieving family who just lost their loved one in such a tragic accident less than 24 hours ago. And you actually expect that your questions will be answered! Eventually my brother and sister talked to the reporters, because Robert and I refused to. It just amazed me how some people can be so disconnected, self-centered, and disrespectful. I understand they have a job to do, but I believe they should at least ask your permission before arriving to your doorstep. All of this was nothing compared to the craziness that was sure to come later.

Later on in the day we receive a call letting us know that the students and staff of D'Ashawn's high school would like to have a vigil at 6pm that evening in his honor, they wanted to know if we felt up to attending. I truly did not feel up to doing anything besides burying myself under the covers to never come out again! But of course I couldn't do that. I absolutely agreed to attend. My son would have wanted it that way, plus I felt it was the least I could do to show my appreciation for his high school family and all those impacted by my son in some way, shape, or form. To my amazement, we arrive to a parking lot filled to capacity! The vigil takes place on the football field and the score board is lit up with the number *43* all over it, which was my son's football number. There are so many people that for a moment I actually tune out the real reason we are all there because I am in awe! I cannot believe that all these people showed up for *MY SON! MY D. LEW! MY BABY!* Even though it was very emotional, the vigil was absolutely beautiful! I was so emotionally exhausted at the end, all I can remember saying is "I want to go home!" The news reporters, who took beautiful pictures by the way, lurked outside the gates, they weren't allowed onto the field. They would report the next day that over 600 people attended the vigil of a senior football player fatally wounded the day before walking home from track practice. Over 600 people??!!! For my son??!! Why? How? I had no idea the amazing impact this young man had on so many people! After all, he was just D'A to us! The one who danced every minute of the day when he wasn't playing football or talking about football, just our D'Ashawn who we laughed with, debated with, ate with, and most of all, loved dearly! That ride home from the vigil had me in such a confused space. Deeply grieving over the loss of my son, but also rejoicing because of the amazing acts of kindness I had just witnessed. Only *GOD* could allow something of that magnitude to take place. So many people, so many young men crying like babies, I had never seen anything like that before in my life! The entire night we just sat in amazement. Just reflecting and trying to process that this amazing night was all for our *D. Lew!*

*Friday,
December 2, 2011*

I woke up today and it hit me, my usual routine of waking my son for school was no more. Instead, I had to begin the daunting task of planning his home going services. I'm so numb at this point; all I can focus on is just getting this all over with so I can try to get back to what is left of my life. It's only the third day, and I'm emotionally, physically, and mentally drained. I can't remember the last time I've eaten so my mother and sister decide to take me to my favorite breakfast spot, *"The Waffle House."* They wanted me to try and eat something and try to get a mental break from all that was going on. I must admit, that short time away from the chaos that was my life was well needed. Thankfully we didn't run into anyone that knew us personally, although I still felt like a fish in a fishbowl. Like everyone knew I was the mother of the 17 year old kid who had just been hit by a car and killed. Again, I'm a very private person, so this is all very overwhelming for me, trying to grieve while having everyone's eyes on you is a lot to deal with. We got the call stating D'Ashawn had been picked up by the funeral home, so at 12 noon we arrive to start planning his home going. Through this process I learned that people may mean well, but can add more stress to an already stressful situation. The five of us arrive at the funeral home, Robert, my mother, my sister, my grandmother, and I. My plan is to make these decisions as quick as possible and get to the cemetery to complete everything. To my surprise, this turned into an all-day process. I had no idea how much time it would take to get these things taken care of! Everyone has ideas on what they think is best, but this isn't everyone's son, this is my son! And I plan to send him away the way I want! Again, people may mean well, but it is very frustrating when you actually have to do the hardest thing in life, and you have people wanting to debate and make demands on which casket, which flowers, and which colors! The casket I chose was absolutely perfect!! Black and gold, a direct representation of his high school colors, red roses were chosen for his flower arrangement, red was his favorite color. The funeral date is set for the following Thursday, December 8, 2011. I tried to push that date up, but it was impossible, again, I wanted this to all be over! With everything completed at the funeral home, we all head to the cemetery. My preference is to have him placed in a mausoleum, but of course my family has other ideas! My family has several plots at this cemetery and preferred he be buried next to other family members. I can appreciate that, but again, I am his mother, and I did not want him in the ground! I wanted him in a place away from the elements of the earth. But because the available spaces for the mausoleum were very high up, I chose to just place him in the ground. Being there, at the cemetery, put Robert and I in a very solemn place, we had just gone through this same thing at the beginning of 2011. It makes you ask yourself, "Is this real?" "Do we really have to go through this again?" It's amazing where you can find yourself not even a full year later!

"I will say of the Lord, He is my refuge and my fortress; my GOD; in him I will trust."

(Psalms 91:2 KJV)

The first three days are over! Even though a date has been set, the first obituary notice for the newspaper has been written, and the arrangements have been finalized, it still hasn't sunk in. It's like I'm physically here, but not mentally. It's like time is moving in super slow motion. The next thing on our list is to visit the person who will be making the programs for the home going services. I tried to prepare myself by making sure I had the appropriate names written down so that I wouldn't miss anyone. We were also told to bring any photos we may want to appear in the program. I would later realize that after all of that prep work, I still forgot one of the most important people in both D'Ashawn's and my life, my best friend of over twenty years! She was my son's godmother of course, but he always called her his "fairy godmother!" How on Earth could I forget her??!!! How?? I felt like the most horrible person in the world! I didn't realize it until after the funeral and it weighed so heavy on my heart! I asked that she not blame it on my heart, blame it on my mind. So much was going on that it had completely gotten pass me. But I promised to make it up to her. And as always, I kept my word! Not too long after everything settled down, and I had begun an attempt to get back to my life, I reached out to the person who made those programs for us. Luckily, she still had it on file and was able to add in my best friend's name!! I was ecstatic that I could make things right. After all, she is only my best friend and D.Lew's *"fairy godmother"*, she surely deserved her recognition!

As the days drag on, all I can think about is that I'm so ready to get through all of this and try to piece my life back together. The arrangements have been finalized, and his high school has been so supportive and accommodating. They've honored every single request, no matter how big or small. My son loved his school, he loved his band, and he especially loved his athletic family! The overwhelming support from everyone is what made this time in my life just a tad bit easier! I wanted his home going service to reflect every aspect of his life, all the people, places, and things that he loved! I wanted him to be proud of me. I wanted to pay homage to the life of the only man who stole my heart! How? How do you prepare yourself to bury your one and only child? Any child for that matter! Where do you find the strength to endure all that comes with losing a child? It still amazes me to this day; I'm amazed that I made it through. People always say that I'm "so strong". I let them know that it is not me; it's my faith that strengthens me!!

"Wait on the Lord: be of good courage, and he shall strengthen thine heart: wait, I say, on the Lord." (Psalms 27 v. 14)

My faith in *GOD* is why I have survived! I was blessed with a very strong support system and faith that told me that I was only as strong as the *GOD* I serve. Any obstacles put in front of me were for a purpose, and he would give me what I needed to overcome them. Having faith at this time in my life was necessary. There are so many who experience these same life events and are not able to cope. They may not have support or a religious background, so they don't believe in faith or a higher power. Or they may believe in a higher power, but may not understand why they have been forsaken. Not once did I ever question why, why my son, or why me. Not once!! My faith wouldn't allow me to. I had to understand that my son came here for a purpose; he served that purpose, and has now earned his wings.

"I can do all things through Christ who strengthens me."

(Philippians 4 v. 13)

*Tuesday,
December 6, 2011*

Today is the day! Today is the day I finally get to see my son. Today is the day I get to view him, approve how he looks, and come face to face with my reality. He's actually gone……forever! I arrive at the funeral home and for some reason, I'm not nervous. To my surprise, my family is already there. I really wanted to do this alone. I understand why they are there, but it's a bit overwhelming. So I ask that they allow me to go in alone first, and then they can go in afterwards. I walk in, and I feel somewhat relieved. Maybe because I hadn't seen him in what has now been six days, and I had no idea what he'd look like or what condition he would be in. He looks amazing!! He looks peaceful and just as handsome as ever! It may sound crazy, but I was happy. My spirit had been calmed; I guess I just needed to lay eyes on him. He looks so nice, especially his haircut! He was always very particular about his haircut, and it was absolutely perfect! He looked so at peace, so still, as if it were the soundest sleep he'd ever had. In that moment, I stood there, just fixated on him. It felt as though every moment of his entire life had flashed before my eyes, so many emotions in just that brief moment, it was as if time stood still. I sent him home wearing a crisp white dress shirt, black dress pants, and his high school football jersey. Again, the school accommodated each and every one of my requests, and I will forever be grateful for that. Not only did they allow me to bury him in his jersey, each of his team mates signed a souvenir football for him that I still proudly display in my home. Their generosity and willingness to help will forever be appreciated!

wearing a crisp white dress shirt, black dress pants, and his high school football jersey. Again, the school accommodated each of every one of my requests, and I will forever be grateful for that. Not only did they allow me to bury him in his jersey, most of his teammates signed a solid white football... him that day, ready to go home with him. Their generosity and ... ... on that day will forever be appreciated.

*Wednesday,
December 7, 2011*

Today he is available to the public for viewing. I have chosen to stay home today and not visit the funeral home. I really wanted to stay away from all the commotion that was sure to take place. So many people coming to pay their respects and say their goodbyes, I just wanted to try and find some sort of peace today. I needed to give myself a mental break and somewhat prepare for the home going services the next day. So many people are affected by a tragedy such as this, even people who don't know the family or the victim. It's one of those things you hear about and say "I can't imagine what that family is going through. I've said that, I've heard tragic news and wondered "how are they going to cope?" Saying to myself, "I would just die" or "I couldn't make it through that". But in that moment, as I was going through the tragedy of a lifetime, none of that crossed my mind. I was in a complete fog, people coming and going, calls, text messages, cards, food deliveries, running errands here and there, deciding which flower, which casket, it was just all too much! You never realize how you will react to something until you go through it. People can comfort you and have the best intentions, but to actually be the one going through all the aspects of something of this nature, words could never explain that feeling. It's something I wouldn't wish on my worst enemy. By the grace of *GOD* I remained sane enough to make it through.

through all the aspects of something of this nature, words could never explain that feeling. It's something I wouldn't wish on my worst enemy, by the grace of GOD I remained sane enough to make it through.

*Thursday,
December 8, 2011*

I woke up this morning in a complete daze. This is it, today is the day. Today is where my son's flesh can find peace and I can send him on to a much better place. Services begin at 11am. Around 9:30, my family starts to arrive. Everyone plans to line up and all leave from my home. Around 10 the funeral directors arrive, give us instructions, and pray with us before we begin the funeral procession. I climb into the family car still in shock, an entire week later! "Am I really about to do this?" "Am I really on my way to MY son's home going services?" They say funerals and weddings are when people act the craziest, which would prove to be all too true for me today! We arrive at the church and all I could think was, "Are all these people here for the D'Ashawn?" The parking lot was filled as if it was time for Sunday service! I could not believe it! So many people, some who didn't actually know him personally, but just wanted to pay their respects. There were so many levels of emotion running through me as we sat in the car waiting for the funeral directors to guide us inside the church. All of the immediate family members are assembled in the smaller sanctuary to line up for the entrance into the main sanctuary. They call our names based on the order in which they are listed on the program. First the parents, siblings, great grandparents, grandparents, uncles, aunts, etc., we line up and head to the main sanctuary to walk in. As we're waiting in line, I hear some commotion behind me, but I'm not clear on what is going on, and I'm clearly not in my right mind, so I pay it no attention. It's time, time for us to walk in. I look straight ahead and there he is. My one and only, the first love of my life! It was almost like I had tunnel vision. All I could see was him lying there, in a peaceful sleep. For some reason I feel like everyone is waiting for me to crack, like waiting for me to just roll down the aisles hollering and crying. That's how I feel inside, but of course I don't do that. I approach the casket and I just stare at him. I see him, he's lying there, but it still doesn't seem real. He looks so peaceful. As if he just fell into an eternal sleep. It's the most heart wrenching feeling ever! To look down on a life you created, gave birth to, raised, nourished, and now have to bury. How do you do that? How do you look down to your child, your one and only son lying in a casket? My only answer is, it was not me, it most definitely my faith! I haven't always been as connected to my faith in *GOD* as

I should have been, but the foundation I never forgot. I've always understood from whom my blessings flowed.

"Cast they burden upon the Lord, and he shall sustain thee: he shall never suffer the righteous to be moved." (Psalms 55 v.22)

I believed in my faith and trusted in Christ knowing that *he* was the only way that I would survive this! The hurt I felt then is the exact same hurt I still feel as I write this! I sat through his entire home going service in a complete fog, completely unaware of all that was going on around me. I was there physically, but mentally I was somewhere else. Even during the service I found myself concerned with the well-being of my family. I held it together for them; I just wanted everyone to be okay. The music, the singing, the eulogy, the condolences, the memorial video, it was a home going service fit for a king! I found myself looking over the church, in amazement. I looked to my right and I saw the entire football team dressed in their jerseys and crying so hard they could hardly compose themselves. I looked down my row of seats and saw the devastation and hurt on the faces of children that lost their brother, I watched the memorial video and couldn't believe that his life was over. I listened to my aunt read the cards, prayers, and acknowledgements and she could barely speak because she was so full of grief and heartache. You see it, you hear it, you feel it, but yet, it is still unreal. The service ends and we head to the cemetery. As he reaches his final resting place, his high school band begins to play for him one last time. The band members are so overwhelmed with grief, they can hardly focus! They found their strength to fight through the tears and honor their school mate one last time! The graveside service ends and people start to congregate before heading to the church for the repast. Before I can get in the car to head back, I start to hear small talk about certain family members who've been voicing their opinions about how certain things were handled for *MY* son's home going services. I get in the car, and the entire ride home, I'm just in utter shock! I get home, and yet again, the same thing, I'm hearing that some felt they should've sat here or there, their name should have been listed here in the obituary, I should have done this, I put these person/persons ahead of my family. Like really?? Is this what people are focused on? Are people this shallow and selfish that instead of them acknowledging the fact that I just buried my son, they would rather concern themselves with their own unimportant, irrelevant wants and needs? I just couldn't believe that people could be so disrespectful! Not just people, my family! The ones I trusted and stood by, the same ones who should have been standing by me during this nightmare. When I confronted them, of course not one of them felt there was any type of fault in their actions. They were argumentative and felt as though their actions were justified. This is how I knew that every word of what was told to me was absolutely true, and they could care less about what really mattered at the time, my son! I later found out that the commotion I heard while in line waiting to enter the sanctuary were those same family members cursing, complaining, yelling, and not only disrespecting a holy place, but disrespecting my son, themselves, and what those who loved him were really there for, to peacefully say our final goodbyes. Before anything, family is supposed to be there in your time of need! It amazed me that during that time in my life the one person I could trust and lean on was no longer with me! Still, as I write this, I still cannot believe or understand a person who could be so thoughtless and disrespectful, so childish and disgustingly selfish! Needless to say, those relationships have forever been changed! Sometimes you have to learn to love people from a distance. Some may believe that you are supposed to stand by people regardless of what they do. I believe that family is supposed to stick together. I don't have that, and I'm okay with that. The relationships may be strained, but that doesn't mean that I love them any less. I just know what my boundaries are and what I need to do to progress in my own life. Through this journey, I've realized that unfortunately, family is not as loyal and trustworthy as they should be. I've built relationships with those who are not blood, but who have stood by me more than my real family has. Not everyone is wired the same, not everyone understands the true meaning of family, loyalty, or what it means to be supportive and to sometimes put the needs of others above those of your own. As I grow older, I understand that. I understand that not everyone will think the same way I do, not everyone has the same heart, and that's okay. When you learn this, you learn that you have to pray for those who may be on a different path than yourself, love them from a distance, and be at peace within your own existence.

I would like to give a special thank you to those who helped to make his home going service special! I love and fully appreciate those who extended themselves in some way, form, or fashion. His high school football team who carried him all the way to the end, the cheerleaders who carried his flowers, the band who played for him, those who spoke over his spirit, prayed for us, and some who didn't even know us, yet showed tremendous amounts of support. Please know that I carry it with me at all times!

The Day After

The day after, the day I attempt to figure it all out and try to piece my life back together. How? How do you do that? How do you move forward without the one piece of your heart that gave you the reason to live in the first place? In my head, I know it's real, I know it happened, but I'm still in a fog! In my mind I rushed to get through this process, not realizing it would bring me to this point where I don't know what my next move should be. I decided to create *"The D. Lewis Foundation"* to honor my son. Initially it was created to give back to his high school family that gave so much to him. But slowly it has begun to grow. Through donations and the support of the community, we were able to give two book scholarships to two students from my son's 2012 graduating class! That was a great accomplishment for our first try! Since then, the foundation has done food drives for Thanksgiving, participated in gathering donations for an annual event held for the homeless, and continued book scholarships for graduating seniors at his high school. All of this has helped me make it through my grief! There's a lot I miss out on because my son is no longer with me. Thankfully, his graduation wasn't one of those things. The school decided to honor him by draping his seat with a cap and gown and allowing me to walk up and receive his diploma on his behalf! Even though it was hard to do, I was honored to do it!

The Aftermath

Day by day, I find myself sinking. On the outside I appear to be handling everything so well, but in reality, I'm dying! I'm here physically, but not mentally. Everyone seems to think that I'm so strong; they just don't know that I'm dying on the inside! They don't know that I'm slowly losing myself in my current existence. Settling in a dysfunctional personal life, all while knowing that I don't belong here. Wanting nothing but to hear my son's voice, see his face, receive a text message from him, or to see him dance across the floor one more time! During this entire ordeal, I've managed to hold it together, to not allow the outside world see me break down. Why you ask? I don't know. I just always felt like people were waiting for me to crack, waiting for me to fall apart. I also didn't want those closest to me to lose it. I felt like I had to stay strong for them, like if they saw me "have a moment", they would become overwhelmed with emotion. The day I had to choose and design my son's head stone, that all came to an abrupt end! I went into the office of the memorial company and let them know why I was there, I went in alone. They directed me to a field outside where they have all the displays and samples of the memorials and head stones. My mother and grandmother rode with me, but I told them that I wanted to do this alone. Well, they saw me walking into the field and decided to join me. So many options, so many different types and stone colors, it was overwhelming! I paced back and forth, in a daze. I was so undecided on what it should say or what it should look like, wanting nothing but perfection for my son. And then, in an instant, I lost it!! I lost all emotional control!! I turned around to my mother and grandmother standing behind me, and it was all over their faces, FINALLY! I let it all out! Even writing this right now I have anxiety because I can still feel the intense pressure of that moment. It's like buying that headstone was confirmation. Like up until that point it wasn't real. I was inconsolable. I hadn't released any major emotion since the night this nightmare began. Everyone around me was so supportive, even the people who worked at the memorial company. They offered me the opportunity to come back, but I wanted to get it done that day! That is not something I could stand to do twice. I took my time and designed something I thought my son would be proud of. Every step, every decision, everything to this day has been done with respect to his memory and honor on his name. I realized that in order to begin healing, I needed to separate myself from the current chaos that was my life. Seven months after the loss of my son, I moved on from the man I was supposed to marry, and started to focus on Nicole!

Me, Myself, & I

This loss has forever changed me! It's forced me to look at things with an entirely different mindset. The opinions and cares of others are no longer cares of mine. I started a new job and tried to focus more on myself. Time has passed, and it has now been a little over a year since the accident. The moments of loneliness continue. The times where I break down and scream and cry my eyes out continue. The fog has not been lifted, it has gotten thicker. I'm alive, but am I living? I decided to start seeing a counselor. Maybe I need some help to cope with all that I'm feeling. It has taken me a year, but better late than never. I see the counselor, and after two visits I have some clarity over my situation. She helped me to understand why I have reacted to this tragedy in my life so coldly. Why I've been so shut off and private. I try to use the tools given to me by the counselor to improve my life and how I function in it. But as time goes on, I'm becoming more and more secluded. I've turned into a robot, work and home, work and home. No dates, no nights out with the girls, no time with family, just me, myself, and I.

As I continue to struggle with what my life is supposed to be, I run into yet another obstacle. In 2013 I began to have problems with my menstrual cycle. It's very heavy and painful. It seems to worsen over time, and around August 2013 I see my doctor about it. She does an ultrasound and advises me that I have fibroid cysts; these are the reason for the changes I've been experiencing. With each cycle, the blood flow causes the cysts to enlarge. So by August, they are pretty huge. She decides on a less invasive procedure first to rectify the issue. She preps me for the procedure; it required mild sedation, and proceeds to remove the cysts. As she goes in, she realizes that the cysts are attached to a major artery. Because of this, she is unable to complete the procedure. I awaken thinking that it is all over with. To my surprise, nothing was done. She showed me a photo of the cysts and how they were positioned and advised me that if she attempted to remove them, I could have bled out, and ultimately bled to death. Unfortunately because of that, her only course of action was a partial hysterectomy. A young, unwed, 34 year old woman, who lost her only son, is now losing her option to have more kids. She stated the partial hysterectomy was the best option due to the fact that I would still have my ovaries; she felt a full hysterectomy was too extreme for someone my age. All of this was very overwhelming, but I knew that it was my only option. I couldn't continue to go through each month with that excruciating pain and heavy bleeding. I dealt with this the same way I dealt with the loss of my son. It was *GOD*'s will, I had to stay faithful and trust that he had a better plan for me. I've had to learn that what I have planned for my life is not always what he has planned.

"Trust in the Lord with all thine heart; and lean not unto thine own understanding. In all thy ways acknowledge him, and he shall direct thy paths." (Proverbs 3 v. 5-6)

I have the partial hysterectomy done in October of 2013, and I have to stay in the hospital for a few days, it was honestly the most restful few days ever!! I don't think I can ever remember sleeping so well. I'm not sure if it was the medication, or just being away from home, but it was very peaceful. I return to work after about two weeks and once again, try to get on with my life, try to make the best out of a bad situation. The holidays are approaching, and as always, this is a tough time for me. Nothing is the same anymore, the family is different, and we're missing something. It's as if the life we all knew before ended the very moment the accident took place. There are no more Sunday dinners at my grandparents' house and the holidays are no longer full of food, happiness, and family. When we are all there, the vibe is off. We aren't smiling, enjoying one another, or excited about being together. We're missing a piece to our puzzle.

Stuck In Grief

Fast forward to the end of 2014 and I realize that it's been three years since the accident, three years that I haven't lived, that I've just existed. As the New Year approached, I decided I would travel more. I would do my best to ease my way out of this box I'd built around myself. I decided to live more, be more open, and allow people in! January 2015, I went on a four day Disney cruise! I started my year off right! After that, every chance I got, I hit the road! From Charlotte, NC to South Beach, FL! Though I moved about and became more social, I still fell into a slump. The holidays are always a super tough time for me. The anniversary of the accident is November 30th, my birthday is December 11th, of course Christmas is December 25th, and my son's birthday is February 10th. So those few months are always hard for me. As Thanksgiving 2015 approached, I already had it set in my mind that I was going to stay home in bed the entire holiday. I knew I'd be off from work both Thanksgiving Day and "Black Friday", so I planned to stay in bed until that following Monday when it was time to return to work. I did exactly that. I answered no calls or text messages. I watched the annual Thanksgiving Day parade alone, and I barely ate for four days, no visitors, just me, a television, and four walls. My birthday comes, then Christmas, and shortly after, I realize that I'm depressed. I start to concentrate more on my faith, and for New Year's Eve, I vow to make some changes. I know, its cliché, but it is so very true! I went to church New Year's Eve; I hadn't been in the sanctuary of that church since the funeral in December 2011! Even then I stayed away from the lower part of the sanctuary; I decided to sit as far away as I could, so I sat in the balcony. Some may say that sounds crazy, but it was my life, and still is to some extent. Just the thought of sitting anywhere near where I sat on that solemn day sends my anxiety into overdrive.

I knew things needed to change; I just wasn't clear on how to make those changes. I wanted something different for my life. I know my son wouldn't want me to live the way I had been, which was not living at all! I took a vow of celibacy, which was pretty easy because there were no prospects anyways, and I did my best to cleanse emotionally and physically. I wanted to remove all those things that held me down and didn't provide growth or progress. Thoughts, emotions, relationships, people, I needed to start anew, on a more spiritual journey to find myself. In January of 2016, I decided to revisit my counselor. During the first visit, she told me that I was "stuck" in the grieving process. I said "stuck?" She said, "Yes, you are still where you were in 2011. You've put people, situations, and circumstances before yourself. You have to let go! You cannot heal when everyone else is a priority." I left that meeting in awe! That was the most life changing hour of my life since the start of this tragedy!! She opened my eyes and mind in so many ways! She read me like a NY Times best seller! She said there is always a child who takes on the "responsible" role, and I was that child. I sat back and looked over all of the relationships of my life, and she was right. From men to family members, I played the "responsible" role. By doing this I placed myself in a space where I take care of the issues and problems of others. So much so that I literally make them my own! How can one live a normal, functioning life of their own like that? They can't!! I begin to instantly make changes in my life. In this process I've learned that not everyone will agree, and that is okay, that is not your cross to bear! When you begin to make positive changes for your own life, not everyone will approve or agree. But that is their opinion, not yours. Not everyone is supposed to come along for the ride. This change will hurt, because the majority of the time, the ones you need to let go of, are the ones you love the most. We also have to understand that we are not made to have "relationships" with everyone. Some people we encounter, we only need to be cordial with. We don't always need to try to build relationships of some sort with every person in our lives just because they have this role or that role. Once we understand where to place certain people in our lives, we can better understand ourselves and the role those people should be playing.

Finding Purpose,

In My Pain

In an effort to take back my life, I started to pray more, read the bible more, and just positively feed my spirit. I instantly began to see things changing! I know not everyone reading this reads the bible or worships the same, or worships at all for that matter. But whatever your spiritual path may be, be faithful to that. Pray, meditate, read, study, and continuously feed your spirit. Throughout this entire journey, this is what I always go back to, it is my foundation! When you endure any trials in life, you must turn to what gives you solace spiritually! You cannot endure all the hits that life delivers without something to fall back on! IT IS IMPOSSIBLE! And clarity is as simple as having a conversation with Christ.

Two weeks later, I see my counselor for a follow up visit. She is overjoyed by the enormous progress I have made! I took everything from our last meeting to heart and made a promise to myself to act on it. In doing so, I saw a huge change in my life, a change within myself, and a change in how I interact with others, even a change in how others reacted to the "new" me. I began to see the "true colors" of those around me. I began to see how my need to always "take care" of everyone before myself was actually hindering them from being responsible themselves, while also keeping me from progressing forward, how crazy is that! If you do not open the door for foolishness, there is no way for it to enter into your life! When you don't make room for those things that "take away" instead of "add" to your life, you leave room for all the positive thoughts and people who will inspire you, encourage you, and speak favor over your life! During this journey, as I began to remove all that clouded my thoughts, my spiritual space began to widen. The spirit spoke to me at 6 am on February 9, 2016, the day before my son's birthday, and said just as clear as a bell, "you need to write a book". I was so overwhelmed, I began to cry inconsolably! I sent a text to a dear friend, for some reason it was on my heart to text her first, and she was so encouraging! After her, I only told two other individuals. They all confirmed for me what the spirit had already placed on my heart! In that instant, I realized I had finally found my purpose! All this time, I always wondered what my purpose was. I absolutely love being a hairstylist, but for some reason I always knew that was my passion, not my purpose. I never understood that until that very moment! From then on, I decided to tell my story. Sometimes we go through things and deal with them in our own privacy, not realizing that we can possibly help and encourage someone else with our story. I'm a very private person. But I realized this is a part of the challenge. I believe this is why this task has been destined for me. To take me so far out of my box (comfort zone), that I allow myself to reach levels that I couldn't ever imagine; *MY* story could change someone's life, which is amazing! If my story can impact at least one individual, my mission is complete!

March 2016

I continue to pray, write, and focus on making positive changes in my life. In doing this, I was reminded of how my story could impact the world and change so many lives. Those closest to me saw something in me that I had never seen in myself! This is the power of positive thoughts and the result of a spiritual, physical, and emotional cleansing! When you open the doors for positivity, the blessings will flow! You will come across people, places, and things that will amaze you! Find your spiritual guidance and become faithful in it. Find your purpose! Surround yourself with those who speak favor over your life *AND* your purpose! Be encouraged! Remove dead weight, negative energy, negative thoughts, and negative people from your life. When you allow negative feelings and energy to make camp in your spirit, you hinder your growth. You can have great intentions of living a positive life, but if you have not forgiven, if you have not released that anger, and if you have not cleansed yourself of that negative mindset, you will remain stagnant! You cannot progress in life holding on to anger and all those things from your past that have made you bitter and closed off. You have to understand that only *GOD* can fix your heart. Only he can renew your spirit. Fall down on your knees and plead the blood of Jesus over your life!

can renew your spirit. Fall down on your knees and plead the blood of Jesus over your life.

"Elect according to the foreknowledge of GOD the Father, through sanctification of the spirit, unto obedience and sprinkling of the blood of Jesus Christ: Grace unto you, and peace, be multiplied." (1 Peter 1 v. 2)

You must free yourself of those burdens, cleanse your soul, and pray for deliverance. This is how you can refocus and be open to the blessings that are in store for your life. I've learned during this process that I did not allow myself to grieve and move forward with my life because I allowed the issues of others to consume me. *LET IT GO!* Even still, as I write this, I have to tell myself to *LET IT GO!* It is a constant struggle, but it has to be done. Nothing in life is perfect, but if we do not recognize change and become open to it, how can we progress in it? How can we be open to all that life has to offer if we allow things and people who don't add to our lives constantly control it? I will be the first to say that the loss of my son is something that I struggle with every minute of every day. And honestly, I foresee it being this way for the rest of my days, and I am okay with that. When you lose a loved one, whether by death or separation, you have to figure out how to come out on the other side stronger than ever. It will not be easy, but it is necessary for your survival! Find something positive that keeps you sane and grounded. For me, that was my faith and my relationship with Christ. Now, just so there is no confusion, I am in no way claiming to be "holy sanctified" or anything like that. I will always and forever be a work in progress. My *GOD* is not done with me yet. When you open your heart and spirit to positivity, you'll see the changes take place in your life. You will start to see people be removed from your life and you must understand that those people are not meant to continue on with you into the next phase of your journey. During this time, feed your spirit, your mind, your soul and your heart. Take ownership and make peace with any mistakes you may have made in your past. This is critical to your cleansing. A dear friend of mine told me about this awesome thing that she does, which is journaling. She writes everything down that has taken place in her day, good or bad. For over 16 years she has been journaling, so I decided to try it. It is the most freeing thing I have ever done in my life. I have kept a journal before, but I never really took it seriously or was consistent with it. While attempting to move down a more spiritual path, I decided to start journaling again. When you just write, everything flows freely from your mind onto paper, all of your thoughts, ideas, and feelings; all your own, all written in your own words. A recorded history in your own words that you can go back later and read what you've written. I even wrote my prayers in a journal, which is called a prayer journal; it is a conversation with your higher power, just on paper, where you can freely express yourself and draw closer to Christ. Some of us choose not to pray because we don't know how to. A prayer journal is perfect for that! Just simply open your heart and write out your thoughts.

Healing

As I've experienced this tragedy, received counseling, and drawn closer to my spiritual existence, I found that there is a process to healing. There are steps to overcoming what is or has caused you so much pain. This could be divorce, job loss, depression, domestic violence, a disruptive home life, and in my case, the death of my son. What I have experienced doesn't just apply to those of us who have lost children, but to anyone who may have experienced a loss or life event that has taken them into depression, or caused them some type of pain. The first step to redemption is to acknowledge that you are in pain. You must acknowledge the fact that you are still hurting and need help. If you are like me, you are in a fog. You know the tragedy has happened, but you haven't dealt with it. You haven't faced it head on and accepted it as your reality. When you haven't taken accountability for what has happened and how it is impacting you, you are unable to move forward. You will begin to just exist in this world without living. You must accept what has happened and be ready to also accept what comes with it. In my case, I had to accept that my son was now gone and I would never be a grandmother, I would never get to see him graduate high school or college, and I would never get to see him meet the love of his life. So many things I realized I would miss out on because I lost him at such a young age. Those things still affect me today because I see so many of his classmates and friends progressing in life, graduating college, and pursuing their dreams. I have to accept that he won't ever be able to do those things. Although it hurts, I have to understand that I can no longer allow the hurt to consume me. When I feel weak, sad, lonely, and times when I miss him, I pray. I fall on bended knee and ask for guidance and direction. Going back to that dark space is not an option! The same applies to those who are still holding on to anger because their marriage didn't work, their spouse cheated, they weren't chosen for a promotion, or they lost a loved one. You cannot allow that anger to consume you and make you bitter! You will never find happiness still holding on to the past. Anger, grief, bitterness, and doubt are all feelings that weigh you down and keep you from moving forward with your life. How can you fall in love with who *GOD* has for you if you're still angry about someone from your past? How can you be open to receive the blessings laid out for you in your future if you're still grieving over a lost? You must follow the plan of *GOD*! It may not make sense at the time, but everything that has you grieving, angry, and bitter was a part of the plan of *GOD*! It was supposed to happen!!

The next thing is to seek help. You will not be able to win this battle alone, you will need help! You can find help by seeing a counselor or psychologist, talking with your pastor, joining a group with individuals who have had a similar experience as yourself, and reading self-help books or blogs that relate to your situation. As for me, I sought the help of a counselor and also chose to grow closer to my spiritual side and strengthen my relationship with *GOD*. My relationship has always been there, but now was the time that I needed to be devoted to it. I felt that it centered me and kept me sane. As my connection grows, I'm drawn closer to the spirit of *GOD* and I have a better understanding of my life's purpose. I feel that when you strengthen your spiritual connection, no matter the religion, you not only strengthen your spirit, but you strengthen your soul! Your vision becomes so much clearer. You are able to make better decisions for your life and have a better understanding of the things that have taken place in your life.

"Humble yourselves therefore under the mighty hand of GOD, that he may exalt you in due time:" (1 Peter 5 v. 6)

Once you've accepted your reality and are brave enough to face it head on and you've sought out help, you can then take the necessary steps to begin to live your life again. So many things changed for me when I made the decision to get help and take my life back! In doing this, I had to realize that this would not be an overnight fix. Be patient in your progress. Know that just taking the first step is worthy of reward! Not everyone can move forward after grief. Not everyone can come out of the depression caused by their grief. And like me, some get stuck in the grieving process, which is just as bad as not moving at all. Imagine an existence where you look in a mirror and see nothing. There is a body there, but the soul and spirit are absent. You may laugh from time to time, but it's all on the surface. Everything underneath is black, cold, and empty. There is no way you can survive like that. I did it for about four years, four years that I will never get back. Four years of time wasted when I could have been living this wonderfully blessed life *GOD* has bestowed upon me.

We sometimes enter into new phases of our lives without seeking *GOD* first. This is where we make the biggest mistakes. If we're ending one relationship and going into another without first praying for direction, we are bound to fail! Not just romantic relationships, but business relationships as well. We tend to want to make decisions for our own lives, and that is the duty of Christ, not man! When we pray, prayer gives us clarity. It's where we can communicate with Christ, reboot our spirits, and refocus our energy. Then we are able to make decisions with a clearer mindset and we can hear when *GOD* speaks to us. Intimacy with *GOD* requires continuance! In order to remain intimate with the Lord, you are required to continuously seek him! You cannot begin a new chapter in your life still holding on to burdens from past chapters! I could not begin to live in my purpose and understand the anointing on my life still stuck in my grief. Understand me clearly, I will live with this hurt for the rest of my life, but I will no longer allow it to control me! I had to come to grips with my reality and understand the purpose of the pain that I endure. And I say endure because it is still, and will always be a daily struggle for me. But I now understand that my purpose is bigger than my pain! My tragedy was preparation for my triumph!

The moral of the story is, do not allow negative thoughts and feelings, such as anger and doubt to hinder the blessings waiting in your future. You will not find your true purpose holding on to all those things that stunt your growth and stall your happiness. Have you ever wondered why you never get a break or why you haven't found your mate? It's time to do a true self-evaluation, because there is something holding you back. Be honest with yourself! No one can help you if you are not willing to help yourself! It's time to do the work….your happiness depends on it!

Lastly, you have to accept your happiness. Some of us don't know how to be happy after we've gone through a loss. It's okay; it's what *GOD* intended for our lives. The tragedy was supposed to happen to open the doors for the testimony! You have to move on from that dark place and find your happiness. Find what makes you enjoy life again. Find your purpose! I did not find nor understand my purpose until I deepened my spiritual relationship with the Lord. I am still a work in progress and I don't claim to be a prophetess by far, but I do know that my life changed drastically when I drew closer to the Lord. I learned to rely on my spiritual beliefs instead of drowning myself in my grief. It is certainly a process, but it can be done. Sometimes we move on and continue with life with the mindset that this tragedy has happened and that is it. But that's not the case. I am a firm believer that everything happens for a reason. It took me a while to understand what my reasoning was, and that's okay. Again, this is not an overnight process. My nightmare has given me a voice that could potentially help someone who is going through, or has gone through the same thing as I. Someone who may also be stuck in the grieving process, someone who may not understand that they have to find the good in this one thing that is tearing their soul apart, who may not even understand that something good can even come out of something so horrific. You have to survive in your purpose! This means you have to use what has happened in your life as the springboard to the happiness in your future. There is happiness after grief! You can live again, love again, and feel again, you can do it! You can turn things around, it's never too late! I carry the spirit of my son with me knowing that he is watching. I want him to always look down on me and be proud of what he sees. In my case, I feel like I can't let the devil win! There is favor over my life and the Lord has a plan for me. I must follow that knowing my destiny has been ordained! You are the only person who can make a change in your life. Those around you can offer help, hold your hand, and even pray with you, but if you are not willing to do the work and make the changes, happiness will not come!

"For as the body without the spirit is dead, so faith without

work is dead also."

(James 2 v. 26)

Happiness is like the pot of gold at the end of the rainbow. We have storms that are filled with lightening, thunder, flooding, and sometimes even hail, but at the end of it all, there is still that rainbow. When you follow the path of the rainbow, you find that pot of gold, your happiness. Not every day will be easy, but it will definitely be worth it. I have the understanding that this will be a fight I will have to endure for the rest of my days, and I'm okay with that as well. I'm okay with that knowing that I can become a better me while I endure this fight because now I am equipped with the tools I need to positively progress in life. I now know and understand what makes me happy and what I need to do to achieve that happiness.

Happiness is like the pot of gold at the end of the rainbow. We have storms that are filled with lightning, thunder, flooding, and sometimes even hail, but at the end of it all, there is that rainbow. When you follow the path of the rainbow, you will find the pot of gold. Your happiness won't ... be easy, but ... it be worth it. There have been ...

Present Day

I continue to pursue happiness and honor my son in each and everything I do! It still amazes me that even today, almost 5 years later, people still think of him! The social media posts, the tattoos, the dedications, he still lives on. He impacted so many, and I will forever be grateful for that. *GOD* blessed me with the honor and privilege of being his mother, his destiny was ordained. He came, he saw, he lived, he gave, and then his time ended. Though he lived a short life, he lived a *FULL* life! I encourage all who read this to *LIVE LIFE!* Love on your kids, your loved ones, and even your enemies. You never know when that last goodbye or I Love You will be the very last. Make the most of the time you spend here on earth. Change someone's life, give openly, love deeply, take risks, and most of all, have fun! Stay faithful to your beliefs. Expand your spirit and learn to forgive.

"For it is written, As I live, saith the Lord, every knee shall bow to me, and every tongue shall confess to GOD."(Romans 14 v.11)

When you have no one to turn to, you see no light at the end of the tunnel, fall down on your knees and pray! Give *GOD* all the grace and glory he deserves! He is the one and only answer! Stay faithful to him in good times and in bad, you will see the change in your life. By *GOD's* grace I am making it through! It has not been easy, but that is what makes it all worth it. Learn to love on yourself and put your well-being first. It is okay to be selfish sometimes when it comes to your sanity. Sometimes people will unknowingly take, take, and take, not even realizing that they have not considered you at all. But when you allow yourself to be so accessible, you open the door, allowing others to take and feel like they don't ever need to give. I did this for so long and did not realize that I was the major part of the problem! Seek counseling of some sort. Sometimes talking with someone who is not biased and has an open and honest ear can make a huge difference. And last but not least, stay in the fight!!! Don't ever give up! Stay strong in your faith; it will always carry you through. Be persistent in your dream! Remain positive and do not allow yourself to get caught up in the issues of others. Your journey is yours and yours alone, don't waste it!

As for me, my story is to be continued. Thank you for allowing me to share my journey thus far. My future can only brighten from here! I've experienced depression and thoughts of suicide long before losing my son. I was in an abusive relationship with no outside support and my son is the reason why I am still here! At that time, I was a young mother, and because of him, I didn't give up! I stayed strong for my son and I was able to remove myself from that relationship. Find that one thing that motivates you and use it! Let it drive you, encourage you, and allow it to be your saving grace. Just stay in the fight, do not give up, your story is still being written!

Dear reader,

As long as my story is to be continued, thank you for allowing me to share my journey this far. My future can only be taken from here. I've experienced depression and thoughts of giving up. To honor my son, I was...

I have ... side support and my sensations of...

... tell this story

... we will fight for...

... because I'll continue... about...

"So all of us who have had that veil removed can see and reflect the glory of the Lord. And the Lord-who is the spirit- makes us more and more like him as we are changed into his glorious image." (2 Corinthians 3 v. 18)

Nicole Roshelle

The chain you see in this photo was a part of a pre-game ritual for D'Ashawn. Before each game he would listen to his music, salute each team member, and wear this very chain. Some may look at this chain and see something negative; I see something as simple as a chain giving a passionate athlete the drive he needed to win games every Friday night! Not only did he motivate himself by wearing this chain, he made sure to personally motivate each and every member of his team.

FIND YOUR CHAIN!

The D'Ashawn Lewis Foundation was established to create opportunities for the youth and give back to our communities. Please continue to support our efforts as we strive to positively impact the world in honor of D'Ashawn L. Lewis.

Visit us at
www.NicoleRoshelle.com/The-D-Lewis-Foundation
and join our mailing list to receive up to date information on our foundation!

www.ingramcontent.com/pod-product-compliance
Lightning Source LLC
Chambersburg PA
CBHW051943160426
43198CB00013B/2282